how

YOUR

talk about

MIND

your mental health

MATTERS

KATY GEORGIOU

YOUR MIND MATTERS

An Hachette UK Company
www.hachette.co.uk

Vie Books, an imprint of Summersdale Publishers Ltd
Part of Octopus Publishing Group Limited
Carmelite House
50 Victoria Embankment
LONDON
EC4Y 0DZ
UK

www.summersdale.com

Printed and bound in China

ISBN: 978-1-80007-410-1

Substantial discounts on bulk quantities of Summersdale books are available to corporations, professional associations and other organizations. For details contact general enquiries: telephone: +44 (0) 1243 771107 or email: enquiries@summersdale.com.

Disclaimer
This book is not intended as a substitute for the medical advice of a doctor or physician. If you are experiencing problems with your health, it is always best to follow the advice of a medical professional.

CONTENTS

INTRODUCTION

Welcome. Whether you're struggling to cope or could do with some guidance on emotionally supporting someone you love, you've come to the right place. In this book, you'll find tools to help you understand why you're feeling out of sorts, the science behind what's happening and what to do about it. In Parts One and Two, you'll discover just how common mental health issues are, with information on the triggers and causes for the issues you or someone you know may be facing. In Parts Three to Five, you'll learn to arm yourself with resources, and you will find self-help tips and advice on how to access professional help. When it comes to your mental health, realizing that you're not alone is powerful. We're often fed the message, "open up", but knowing who to turn to and where to go isn't always clear. This book will equip you with the confidence to go about getting the help you require.

I am enough.
My heart is enough.

Dolly Alderton

PART ONE
YOUR FEELINGS ARE VALID

So much of what keeps us suffering is the fear that if we open up, we won't be understood. But what you're going through is real, and knowing you're not alone can really help. In this part, you'll get to grips with some of the current scientific, medical and therapeutic thinking around mental health, to help you understand what's really going on for you and leave you feeling less alone and more confident about finding help.

LET'S NORMALIZE THIS

Whatever you're going through, it matters. It's easy to think you are making a fuss, that others have it worse, that the people around you are coping just fine, but according to the World Health Organization (WHO), one in four of us will experience a mental health issue during our lifetime. What this means will differ for everyone, but the kinds of difficulties you might experience include anything from mild, passing sadness off the back of a stressful event, all the way to a chronic, life-long issue affecting your everyday quality of life. Whatever your situation, take it seriously. It can be helpful to know that you are not alone and there are others not too far away who are going through it too.

Current medical thinking divides clinical mental health problems into two main categories: neuroses and psychoses. In this book, you'll discover what those terms mean and find helpful guidance on them both.

The good news is the world is shifting its attitude around mental health, and there has never been a better time than now in terms of what we know and how to help. Take courage in that thought as you move through this book.

You only really need

TWO PEOPLE
TO BELIEVE

in the same thing,
to feel as though you just

MIGHT BELONG.

JOANNA CANNON

I AM WORTHY OF LOVE AND HAPPINESS

FEEL NO SHAME

Life throws us curveballs, such as debt, heartbreak or grief. These bumps in the road can knock us off balance and impact our ability to cope. Other times, our emotions become unregulated because of our past, like a difficult childhood, or because of hormonal changes, such as an underactive thyroid. Sometimes, there is no clear cause for what's happening, but we still develop an issue, much like we could a physical one, such as diabetes or cancer. Precisely what affects us will be down to any combination of chance, genes, hormones and life experiences. None of it is our fault.

Thing to remember
is if we're all alone,
then we're all
together in that too.

Cecelia Ahern

FEEL YOUR FEELINGS

It can be tempting to run from your feelings and always strive to be happy. In a world that values positivity, this is understandable. But ignoring your more complicated side isn't always helpful. There is a difference between dwelling on, ignoring and processing feelings. Think of the difference between picking at a wound, leaving it and tending to it. Picking at it runs the risk of it getting worse, but so can ignoring it. Tending to it with the right kind of care is your best chance of healing. You're far more likely to run into trouble if you don't acknowledge what's bugging you now.

Learning to work through your feelings is a skill, but it has powerful effects.

This book will teach you how to spot where your feelings are coming from, and then how to cope with them. Sometimes this can be done on your own, but other times you might need a friend or someone professional to help. In the following pages, you'll get to understand when to call on which and how.

I DO NOT HAVE TO BE PERFECT

PART TWO
UNDERSTANDING MENTAL HEALTH

In this part, you'll find out about the most common mental health issues and how to recognize them in yourself and other people. You'll learn more about the current thinking behind them, and some tips for working through or tackling them. By the end, you should feel more confident about communicating what you're feeling to people around you, how to spot signs of someone else not coping, and how you can approach them about it, too.

LIFE IS TOUGH, BUT SO ARE YOU

NEUROSES vs PSYCHOSES

The International Classification of Diseases (ICD-11) categorizes mental health disorders into two groups: neuroses and psychoses. With neuroses, you're in touch with reality even if you're struggling, like in anxiety and depression, while psychotic symptoms involve losing touch with reality, like hearing voices, hallucinating or experiencing mania. The following pages will explain all of these things. If you think you're experiencing psychoses, or you're worried about someone, there will be some support here for you.

Warning: it's normal to see ourselves in most disorders – it doesn't mean you have them. This part should help you identify symptoms, but only medical doctors can diagnose you.

NORMAL IS NOTHING MORE THAN A CYCLE ON THE WASHING MACHINE.

WHOOPI GOLDBERG

STRESS AND BURNOUT

Stress accompanies most mental health issues. Acute stress has a clear cause and end, like taking an exam: once the exam is over, so too is the stress. But sometimes we can become chronically stressed because of difficult circumstances, like facing a divorce. Chronic stress can take its toll on us physically and mentally in serious ways, leading to burnout and increased risk of cardiovascular or autoimmune disease. If you've also experienced traumatic events in your life, your stress responses might show up in more complex ways. You will find more details about this towards the end of this part.

FEELING BLUE AND LONELY

Dealing with the Blues

Sometimes we can just feel out of sorts, without it meaning we have a mental health problem. However, if you've been feeling low, irritable, snappy or more teary than usual, resentful of others, or you're experiencing insomnia or other physical symptoms such as breakouts, hair loss or menstrual changes with no clear cause, or you're drinking more or not eating properly, these could be signs to pay attention to your self-care from now, in which case you'll find Part Four helpful. It can be helpful to voice this to people you know. If your feelings persist or are difficult to untangle, counselling can be helpful (see Part Five).

When You're Lonely

Being alone and feeling lonely are very different. You can enjoy your own company, while you can feel isolated in a room full of people. Loneliness happens when we feel disconnected from everyone around us, as if we don't belong. It can affect anyone. The British Medical Journal estimates that a third of the population in industrialized countries experience loneliness. Parts Three and Four should help you understand more about why you feel alone, with some useful, simple tips for creating meaningful connections.

I've GOT this

I learned that
my sadness never
destroyed what was
great about me.

Lady Gaga

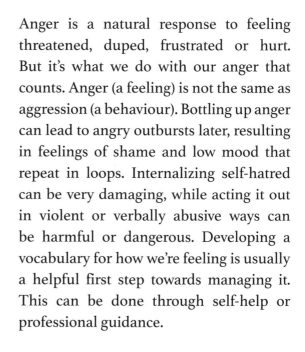

ANGER

Anger is a natural response to feeling threatened, duped, frustrated or hurt. But it's what we do with our anger that counts. Anger (a feeling) is not the same as aggression (a behaviour). Bottling up anger can lead to angry outbursts later, resulting in feelings of shame and low mood that repeat in loops. Internalizing self-hatred can be very damaging, while acting it out in violent or verbally abusive ways can be harmful or dangerous. Developing a vocabulary for how we're feeling is usually a helpful first step towards managing it. This can be done through self-help or professional guidance.

I AM DOING GREAT

DEPRESSION

Depression is complex, with no one clear cause. For some, stressful life events such as divorce can trigger it, while for others, a combination of genes, early life experiences and events over time can build up into a bigger problem. Hormonal changes, medication, drugs and alcohol can be a factor, too. It is more than sadness; you can feel empty, numb or hopeless for days and weeks, affecting your self-esteem. You can rarely just "snap out of it", and being told to can leave you feeling worse. You might feel guilty, hate or harm yourself, or feel you're a burden to loved ones. This can become a vicious cycle. Life can feel pointless, and you might give up looking after yourself, perhaps staying in bed for days or no longer washing. Others paint on a smile and hide their feelings with jokes.

Depression has no clear-cut "look" and is not necessarily linked to your exposure to hardship; in fact, many people feel depressed even if on the surface they have an enviable life. Some clues include crying often, snapping at people or using humour to deflect.

If severe lows alternate with severe, out-of-control highs (mania), this can indicate a type of depression called bipolar disorder.

I WILL NEVER GIVE UP ON MYSELF

I've had a lot of

WORRIES IN MY LIFE,

most of which

NEVER HAPPENED.

MARK TWAIN

UNDERSTANDING ANXIETY

Anxiety is a natural response to uncertainty: if someone shouts "boo" behind us, it's normal to jump out of our skin and for our heart rate to increase. Problems arise when symptoms like this happen without a clear reason, or feel out of proportion to what's happened. Anxiety is a mix of physical symptoms, like palpitations, and "What if?" fears. Usually one triggers the other. When you start pre-empting your symptoms, this paradoxically brings them on, triggering more anxious thoughts in a loop.

Ruminating

With anxiety, it's common to ruminate on a particular theme: getting ill, dying, something bad happening, what others think of you, losing control, etc. This usually coincides with going through important life changes. You might seek constant reassurance or try to control events around you. This can become exhausting. You may get stuck in worry loops, such as worrying about the fact that you're worrying. You'll find tools to support you out of this in Parts Four and Five.

The Diagnostic and Statistical Manual of Mental Health Disorders (DSM V) categorizes anxiety into obsessive compulsive disorder (OCD), health anxiety, generalized anxiety, phobias, panic attacks and social anxiety. You'll read about these next.

OBSESSIVE COMPULSIVE DISORDER (OCD)

OCD is often mistaken for being ultra clean or pedantic, but in reality, intrusive thoughts, images or urges are at the crux of it. They are distressing, unwanted thoughts that pop into your head without warning and don't match your value system. They're usually taboo and have themes running through them – religious, sexual or violent, for example, though there are many, usually linked to your biggest fears. These differ from hallucinations. You will usually attach meaning to these experiences, interpreting them as statements about yourself or what others think of you. You seek reassurance by checking or feeling compelled to do things to stop bad things happening. This can be internal (praying, counting, etc) or external (going to the doctor for check-ups), in the hope that these will safeguard you.

This is common for new mothers (afraid of harming their baby), but can affect anyone, especially if you're going through big life changes. Remember that these thoughts are common and don't mean anything. Knowing that it has a name and clear treatment path can be a relief. Exposure and response prevention therapy (ERP) and cognitive behavioural therapy (CBT) are currently standard approaches recommended to help you to cope with uncertainty. OCD can be isolating, but you don't have to feel alone any more.

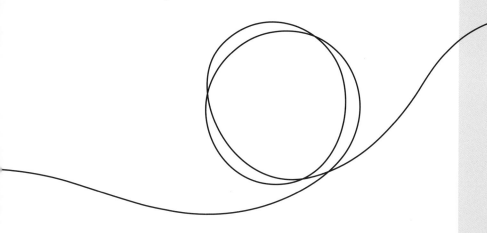

HEALTH AND GENERALIZED ANXIETY

With generalized anxiety, you're feeling anxious about most things, often. It can be difficult to relax, with thoughts buzzing around your brain about everything that could go wrong. You'll usually ask people to reassure you that what's worrying you won't happen, but as soon as one worry is done with, you'll find a new one to think about. Health anxiety is similar, but centres around your health. You might fear developing an illness or interpret common symptoms as signs of serious disease. This can lead to panic attacks or phobias around everyday tasks – like eating, for example.

Phobias are different to everyday fears, in that your efforts to avoid what you're afraid of can dominate your life. When your phobia is around things you won't encounter often (such as snakes or heights), you can mostly work around it. But some phobias have the potential to seriously disrupt your life. Agoraphobia is the fear of being in open spaces or leaving the house, a possible effect of which is that you might stop socializing. A food phobia might start to affect your nutrition and can be linked to other eating disorders.

PANIC ATTACKS

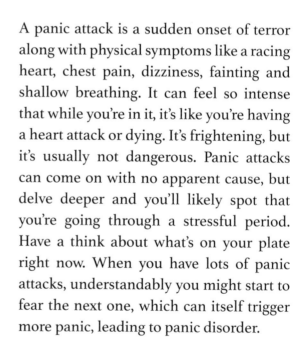

A panic attack is a sudden onset of terror along with physical symptoms like a racing heart, chest pain, dizziness, fainting and shallow breathing. It can feel so intense that while you're in it, it's like you're having a heart attack or dying. It's frightening, but it's usually not dangerous. Panic attacks can come on with no apparent cause, but delve deeper and you'll likely spot that you're going through a stressful period. Have a think about what's on your plate right now. When you have lots of panic attacks, understandably you might start to fear the next one, which can itself trigger more panic, leading to panic disorder.

Mental health... is not a destination, but a process. It's about how you drive, not where you're going.

Noam Shpancer

SOCIAL ANXIETY

Social anxiety disorder is a debilitating fear of being in social situations where you have to interact with people, and this might trigger panic. This could be at a party, meeting friends or even picking up the phone. Symptoms include mulling over conversations you've had, worrying you've offended someone, dreading upcoming events, fearing blushing or making eye contact. Cognitive behavioural therapy is the main method for tackling panic and social anxiety, along with self-help techniques and, in some cases, medication.

RECOVERY IS NOT A RACE

UNDERSTANDING ADDICTION

Habits

You smoke. You're out of cigarettes. You cannot pop to the shops just yet because you've got a meeting, but beyond feeling on edge or irritable, you cope.

Dependency

A detour to the shops will make you late, but you take the risk or cancel because without nicotine, you can't function. Once you've got it, life resumes as usual. This may mean significant interruptions throughout the day.

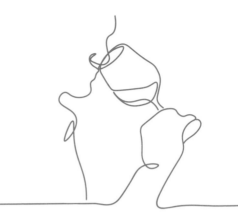

Addiction

What meeting? Your only mission for the day is your fix and everything you do revolves around it, not the other way round. You can be addicted to substances (alcohol, tobacco, drugs) or behaviours (shopping, work, gambling, gaming, sex, porn). This starts as a way of coping but the stakes keep getting higher to reach that same effect. You can end up in debt, lose relationships, your health or your life. Your risk of becoming addicted can be genetic or caused by factors in your environment, such as high stress, unemployment, feeling out of control or being around other people with addictions.

Addiction is treatable. In some cases, such as with alcohol or heroin, quitting suddenly can be life-threatening and requires careful management from trained professionals (see Resources).

POST-TRAUMATIC STRESS DISORDER (PTSD)

Stress is a natural response to trauma, but up to 20 per cent of people who experience trauma develop PTSD, where the experience continues to disrupt your life through nightmares, terror and flashbacks (you relive the experience as if it's happening to you all over again). These symptoms usually develop within three months of the incident and are more likely if you've experienced (or witnessed) war, severe abuse, rape or physical or sexual assault. Studies suggest that the hippocampus in the brain is smaller in people with PTSD, stopping trauma from being processed effectively. Eye movement desensitization and reprocessing (EMDR) or cognitive processing therapy are effective (see Resources).

I DESERVE TO HAVE PEACE.

I deserve to be happy and smiling.

WHY NOT ME?

KID CUDI

COMPLEX PTSD

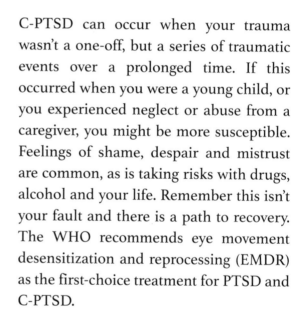

C-PTSD can occur when your trauma wasn't a one-off, but a series of traumatic events over a prolonged time. If this occurred when you were a young child, or you experienced neglect or abuse from a caregiver, you might be more susceptible. Feelings of shame, despair and mistrust are common, as is taking risks with drugs, alcohol and your life. Remember this isn't your fault and there is a path to recovery. The WHO recommends eye movement desensitization and reprocessing (EMDR) as the first-choice treatment for PTSD and C-PTSD.

Be careful not to self-diagnose: consult a doctor or psychiatrist.

I

am

BRAVE

EATING
DISORDERS

There are several types of eating disorder, including anorexia nervosa (not eating), bulimia nervosa (binge eating followed by making yourself sick), binge eating disorder (eating excessive amounts within two hours), or orthorexia nervosa (fixating on the perfect diet, such as clean eating). These are ways of coping with difficult feelings, rooted in finding control in a world that feels so out of our hands. You might be striving for perfection, fear growing up, or want to eliminate feelings like anger and fear from your life. It can be difficult at first to see this as a problem until what starts out as a way of coping ends up feeling like it's controlling you.

SELF-HARM AND SUICIDE

Self-harm

When you self-harm, you're hurting yourself to cope with painful feelings. Usually, it's not about wanting to die, but about turning your emotional pain into a physical one to feel more alive or in control, or to punish yourself. It can give you a short-term release, though over time it can lead to shame and secrecy, which can be lonely. Getting to the source of your emotions, and learning alternative coping techniques to bear your emotions can help you work through this (see Resources).

Suicide

Suicidal thoughts can feel scary, but you'll be surprised by how common they are. They can range from fantasies about death you'll never act on, all the way to making a plan. You might be hiding how you feel from people, or pleading for help. A helpful question to ask yourself is: do you want to die, or stop feeling the way you do? However you feel, research has proven that talking to the right people can alleviate those feelings. Open up to a friend or loved one, or make an appointment with your doctor. There are also helplines and sanctuaries available round the clock wherever you are in the world to support you in confidence.

Call Samaritans free of charge on 116 123, visit nami.org if you're in the US, or try befrienders.org worldwide.

WHEN I HAVE MORE INFORMATION, IT ACTUALLY HELPS ME.

SELENA GOMEZ

I AM
LOVED

MANIA AND PSYCHOSIS

Hearing voices, experiencing delusions or seeing things that others cannot see (hallucinating) can be terrifying, but stigma around these is changing. These symptoms do not always automatically mean psychosis: sometimes they can be triggered by stress, a lack of sleep or illness like the flu, and they can pass. In fact, evidence from the Hearing Voices Network shows that many people hear or see things in their lifetime. However, if these symptoms persist or you're afraid, take them seriously and seek professional medical help. If this is happening to someone you know, encourage them to speak to their doctor.

I
ALWAYS
MATTER

Keep going.
Start by starting.

Meryl Streep

PART THREE
REACHING OUT

It's one thing spotting symptoms, and another knowing what to do about them. In this part, you'll learn how to tell someone how you're feeling, and what kind of help is out there for you. It can be scary opening up when you're vulnerable, especially when you don't know what the outcome might be. But you're doing the right thing in asking for help, and the following pages should help guide you down the right path.

CHOOSING SOMEONE

Identify who in your life you feel the safest talking to. If you're struggling to decide, make a list of people on a piece of paper and notice how you feel as you imagine telling them about this stuff. Are you nervous, cautious, defensive? Do you fear being interrupted, misunderstood or given little attention? These are probably not the people to approach first. Highlight anyone who triggers feelings of warmth and calm. These will be your go-to people. Don't worry if there's no one. We'll get to other routes you can turn to for help.

UNDERSTANDING THE DIFFERENCE

between healthy striving
and perfectionism is critical
to laying down the shield and

PICKING UP
YOUR LIFE.

BRENÉ BROWN

BUILD ON YOUR LIST

In columns, write down the names of:

- People who don't interrupt
- People who can hear difficult things without panicking or making it about them
- People who respect your wishes and don't pressure you to do things their way
- People who have knowledge in the areas you want to talk about
- Wise people you know who give advice you can trust

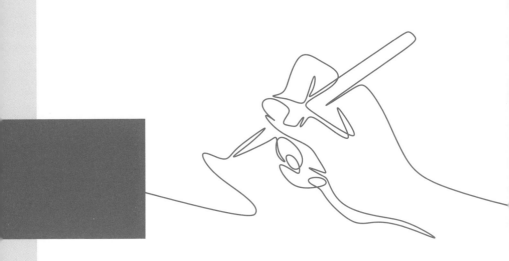

These people do not have to be people you see the most often, or even face to face. Think about your preferred method of contact: in person, by phone, text, Zoom or email? Next to each name, write down their contact details so you can contact them quickly when you need to.

You now have a list ready of people you can turn to for specific things. Keep this list somewhere safe, like in a drawer.

SET YOUR BOUNDARIES

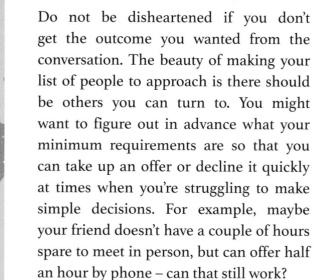

Do not be disheartened if you don't get the outcome you wanted from the conversation. The beauty of making your list of people to approach is there should be others you can turn to. You might want to figure out in advance what your minimum requirements are so that you can take up an offer or decline it quickly at times when you're struggling to make simple decisions. For example, maybe your friend doesn't have a couple of hours spare to meet in person, but can offer half an hour by phone – can that still work?

I WILL NEVER CHANGE WHAT'S BEEN AND GONE

I AM THE ARCHITECT OF MY LIFE

Healing takes time,
and asking for help is
a courageous step.

Mariska Hargitay

STARTING A CONVERSATION

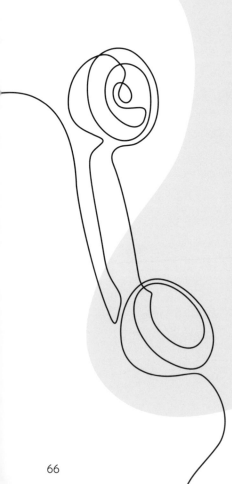

Before approaching anyone, get clear about what you'd like to happen. Make your request specific, with timelines. If you'd like to talk to your best friend for a couple of hours over a coffee, for example, be open about that. Here are some ideas:

"I have something on my mind. Can I call after dinner to pick your brain for a minute?"

Avoid general openers, such as: "Hey, shall we meet up?", which can leave you vulnerable to not getting what you need.

Share your frame of mind and how you need them to be with you:

- "I'm fuming. I could do with a listening ear."
- "I'm in a bad way. I'm not after advice, just someone to hear me out."
- "I'm stuck. Since you work in this field, I could do with some recommendations."
- "I'm not coping. You've been through this before, I figured talking to someone who understands me might help."

Always give a heads up if you're going to share something heavy:

"Something gory happened. Are you OK with me sharing the details?"

This way, the person can let you know if they can offer you what you're asking, without anyone feeling hurt.

DON'T PUT UP OR SHUT UP

Most people are well meaning, but they don't always have the right tool sets for us. When we're low, we can even put up with situations that harm us. If you've taken steps to open up but what's come back doesn't feel right, you don't have to stick with it. Check your list and the other options available to you. In the following pages, you'll find supportive ways to look beyond your immediate support network for help, while in Parts Four and Five, you'll learn some creative self-care tips and how to access more professional, formal support if you need it.

I can

ONLY BE

what

I AM

START WITH
A CHARITY

Going straight to a doctor or professional can feel daunting when you don't know what you're asking for. However, talking to friends isn't always enough. Charities can be a safe middle ground as a first step. They are a great way to connect with others in the same boat, to tap into knowledge and get the intel on road-tested standards of support for your issue. You'll be met with compassion in confidence, alongside trained people who can signpost you to services or offer a listening ear for exactly what you're experiencing. A quick online search for your problem should bring up a list of charities in the area you're looking for.

Nowadays, charity websites are comprehensive, full of information and advice without you even needing to talk to someone. Many also offer free helplines, support groups, community activities and counselling services, or you can simply stop by a branch for leaflets. Plenty of charities also offer one-off drop-in sessions for when you don't need regular support, but you'd welcome someone to check in with every now and then. Opt for trusted charities, like Samaritans in the UK, National Alliance on Mental Illness in the US, Beyond Blue in Australia, Strong Minds in Africa, the Live Laugh Love Foundation in India, or Befrienders Worldwide.

I AM FREE TO CHOOSE

WE NEED TO DO
A BETTER JOB OF
PUTTING OURSELVES
HIGHER ON OUR
OWN TO-DO LIST.

MICHELLE OBAMA

CALL A HELPLINE

When you're struggling and need a soundboard, helplines can be a lifeline. They tend to be anonymous, free to use and confidential, and are available round the clock during hours when more formal services are closed. They are especially helpful in the middle of the night if you can't sleep, for example. They are less formal than counselling and therapy but usually delivered by trained volunteers. Many helplines are available by email, text or instant message, too, to suit your needs. Check what they offer: are you looking for advice, help for a friend, or just someone to listen?

I TRUST
THE WORLD
WILL HELP
ME LIVE MY
BEST LIFE

If we treated ourselves
the way we treated

OUR BEST FRIEND,

can you imagine

HOW MUCH
BETTER OFF WE
WOULD BE?

**MEGHAN, DUCHESS
OF SUSSEX**

SUPPORT GROUPS

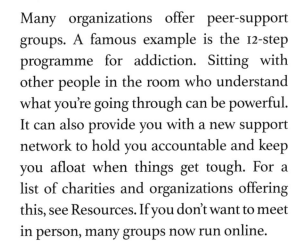

Many organizations offer peer-support groups. A famous example is the 12-step programme for addiction. Sitting with other people in the room who understand what you're going through can be powerful. It can also provide you with a new support network to hold you accountable and keep you afloat when things get tough. For a list of charities and organizations offering this, see Resources. If you don't want to meet in person, many groups now run online.

VISIT
COMMUNITY
HUBS

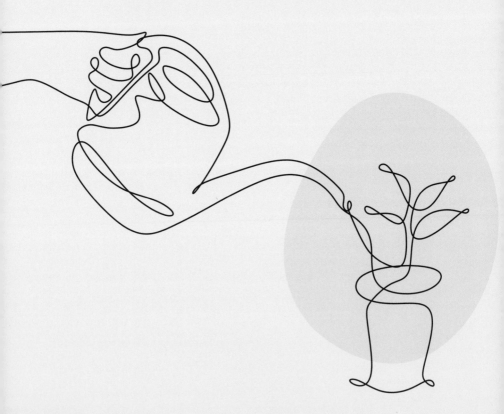

Most local communities have activity hubs – these could be theatre spaces, town halls, churches or charity branches. Search these for social activity, connection and belonging. Many choirs, dance classes and drumming workshops, for example, are set up specifically with support for well-being and mental health in mind. However, there are many communal activities you can take part in that don't have to be about well-being but that give you companionship and purpose, like volunteering for a local allotment or cookery classes. There may also be social gatherings at times of the year like Christmas, Hannukah, Diwali or Eid that are difficult if you don't have family. You can find out all about them by doing an online search for activities in your area, or by visiting your local hotspots where people can help.

MY BODY IS HEALTHY, MY MIND IS BRILLIANT, MY SOUL IS TRANQUIL

The greatest weapon against stress is our ability to choose one thought over another.

William James

My

DIAGNOSIS

does not

DEFINE ME

PEER-TO-PEER NETWORKS

The internet can be a murky place full of misinformation, which is why it can be so helpful to have carefully vetted online peer-to-peer forums to access, such as the Mental Health Forum (mentalhealthforum.net). If you're aged 16–24, the peer networking platform TalkLife is a carefully regulated forum for young people to discuss and explore in confidence any issue from low mood to eating disorders and self-harm. Many have helpful articles, to which you can also contribute.

MAKE USE OF HASHTAGS

Turning to social media can be a quick and useful way to find like-minded people in a similar situation. The @TalkCampus app offers mental health support for more than 80 universities worldwide across 26 languages. The comedian Sarah Millican launched the initiative #joinin. It runs every year on Twitter for anyone spending Christmas Day alone. Simply tweet with the #joinin hashtag throughout the day wherever you are in the world to talk to others in the same boat. If you love music, Tim Burgess from the band The Charlatans runs #timstwitterlisteningparty: he picks an album, and you listen and tweet along with him and everyone else in real time.

Remember: anything you share on social media is public!

HOW
I FEEL
MATTERS

WHAT MENTAL HEALTH NEEDS IS MORE SUNLIGHT, MORE CANDOUR, MORE UNASHAMED CONVERSATION.

GLENN CLOSE

MAKE CONNECTIONS

Cultivating different types of relationship can boost your sense of belonging and add enjoyment to your life. Identify the people who matter to you, and consider any connections you would like but you feel are missing in your life. This could be romantic, sexual or working relationships, or friendships. Think about the places and situations you might find those people in and see if you can take small steps to making those situations happen. If you had connections but you're worried that you've lost touch, don't lose hope. The next page will guide you on how to rekindle relationships with the people you miss.

GET RECONNECTED

Make Micro-Connections

When life gets busy, it isn't always easy to keep in touch. But connections don't have to mean deep conversations; they just need enough to keep them alive. Take pressure off yourself by sending a voice note or calling a friend during the five-minute walk between your home and the train en route to work, school, university or an event, simply to say hello. Or send cards or gifts in the post. These low maintenance micro-connections let people know you're still there.

Connect to Your Purpose

Think about your status in the world, your feeling of purpose, and who you want to be. Are you a brilliant boss but want to start a family? Or a wonderful best friend but wish you had a sibling? We can't fix all of the gaps in our lives, but knowing what they are can help us make sense of how we're feeling. It can be easy to feel shame when we think about what's lacking. The aim of this exercise isn't to make you feel guilty, but to help you understand what really matters to you. You don't have to have it figured out yet.

SHOULD I TALK TO FAMILY?

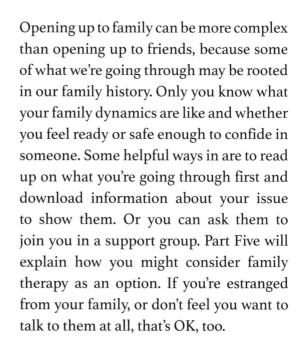

Opening up to family can be more complex than opening up to friends, because some of what we're going through may be rooted in our family history. Only you know what your family dynamics are like and whether you feel ready or safe enough to confide in someone. Some helpful ways in are to read up on what you're going through first and download information about your issue to show them. Or you can ask them to join you in a support group. Part Five will explain how you might consider family therapy as an option. If you're estranged from your family, or don't feel you want to talk to them at all, that's OK, too.

Out of suffering
have emerged the
strongest souls.

Kahlil Gibran

THERE ARE PEOPLE OUT THERE WHO WILL HELP ME

ASK AN AGONY AUNT

Sometimes, anonymity can help us open up. Lots of radio talk shows take calls answering dilemmas without you having to say your name or show your face. You can even listen in to advice being given to others by professionals on air. If you don't like the idea of your voice being heard, try writing in to a magazine agony aunt or consider reading agony aunt pages regularly. Sometimes it can feel like someone else is going through exactly what you're going through.

MARK YOUR "PICK-ME-UP" ZONES

Think about your favourite places in your home. Is it the kitchen, your bed, the shower? Maybe it's the local park down the road, a café that does the best coffee or your favourite street. Make a list of all the places that make you happy. Remembering that you have these places at your disposal to go to when you're feeling blue can help you make choices that you know will lift you.

REACHING OUT FOR SUPPORT SHOWS STRENGTH

You can still

LIVE WELL

with a mental illness.

DEMI LOVATO

CONSIDER THERAPY PETS

Pets can provide great company and companionship. There are also specially trained therapy dogs to help you with specific mental health issues such as panic attacks and depression. They can keep you feeling calm, and give you peace of mind if you're in crisis – many are trained to spot signs of emergency and signal for help. For information on emotional support animals, you can visit www.akc.org/expert-advice/news/everything-about-emotional-support-animals/.

SEEK WORKPLACE OR UNIVERSITY SUPPORT

If you are employed, it's worth checking if your employer has a support scheme in place. Global Employee Assistance Programs provide well-being support for any personal or work-related problem wherever you are in the world and usually include the offer of assessments and counselling sessions. Many workplaces can arrange group coaching or well-being outings, or have external professionals visiting to give talks or workshops. Make the most of these. Your employer may even provide in-house counsellors. If you feel safe enough to confide in a colleague you trust or to talk to your manager about taking some time off or rescheduling your deadlines, take these opportunities.

Most universities have dedicated university counselling services for students, which are free of charge and available to you long term for the duration of your studies. Start by visiting your student welfare office or your university website. You may have to fill in a form.

SUPPORTING LOVED ONES

Even if you're doing OK, listen out for anyone struggling. The signs aren't always obvious. Somebody might tell you they are well, but have they recently lost their job, had their heart broken or moved abroad? If so, check in on them anyway. It could just be a quick text message letting them know they're on your mind. If they do open up to you, always respect their privacy and assume it's confidential. If you're very concerned, the final section of this book contains a list of resources for you to call on for further advice and guidance.

"

Change your
thoughts and you
change your world.

Norman Vincent Peale

"

HOW TO ACTIVELY LISTEN

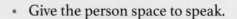

- Give the person space to speak.

- Don't rush to respond. Notice how their words make you feel.

- Ask open questions – the aim is to hear more.

- Try to avoid giving your opinion (unless they ask you for it).

- It can be tempting to want to offer solutions, but don't unless they have asked for advice.

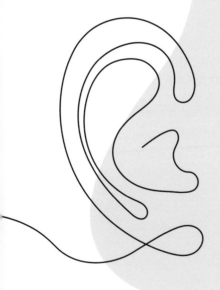

- Focus on feelings, not on what happened. For example, if your friend argued with somebody, go for statements like "How did you feel?" or "What was that like?"

- Reflect how they feel back at them. Show them you've heard.

- Take them seriously if they tell you they're suicidal.

It's OK if you don't have the space to talk. A text message checking in, a photo saying "saw this and thought of you", or a letter in the post can make a difference. This can be helpful when you don't know what to say to help, but you want them to know you care.

VOLUNTARY vs PROFESSIONAL HELP

Most people are well meaning, but not everyone is qualified to help with mental health issues. If the options on the previous pages do not feel enough and you're starting to think you could do with more formal, professional help from a therapist, turn to Part Five. If someone is offering therapy, they should have the appropriate level of training, be registered with a professional regulatory body and behave ethically. You'll learn who's who in the mental health profession, with tips for accessing their help. In the meantime, the next part, on self-care, includes tips on how to help ground yourself in those moments you're on your own.

I AM
WORTHY
OF LOVE

NOTHING CAN DIM THE LIGHT THAT SHINES FROM WITHIN.

MAYA ANGELOU

Almost everything
will work again if you
unplug it for a few
minutes, including you.

Anne Lamott

PART FOUR
MINDFULNESS AND SELF-CARE

Ancient Athenians had a saying, *"kalos kai agathos"*, which means "A healthy body in a healthy mind". The understanding was that your mind and body cannot work without one another. As well as building up strength through physical exercises, people also exercised their minds through debate. In the following pages, you'll find well-being tips for looking after your body, and some recommended self-care activities that work to build both mind and body.

CULTIVATE ROUTINE

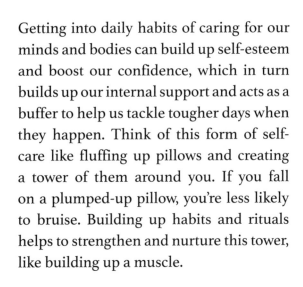

Getting into daily habits of caring for our minds and bodies can build up self-esteem and boost our confidence, which in turn builds up our internal support and acts as a buffer to help us tackle tougher days when they happen. Think of this form of self-care like fluffing up pillows and creating a tower of them around you. If you fall on a plumped-up pillow, you're less likely to bruise. Building up habits and rituals helps to strengthen and nurture this tower, like building up a muscle.

I HAVE MANY POSITIVE THINGS IN MY LIFE

KEEP BREATHING

A simple route to mind and body care is through mindful breathing. This is especially helpful in a panic attack. Taking oxygen into your lungs helps to keep your blood circulating, while focusing on your breath can keep you calm, moving your mind away from your thoughts and into your body. With your feet on the ground, inhale deeply as if you're sucking air up from the ground through your legs. Hold for five seconds, then exhale slowly, picturing your breath leaving your arms and fingertips. Repeat several times. This will be your go-to exercise any time you're having a wobble.

Take care of

YOUR BODY.

It's the only
place you have

TO LIVE.

JIM ROHN

INHALE,
EXHALE

STAY GROUNDED

When you're overwhelmed, panicking or dissociating (feeling detached from your body, disconnecting from your thoughts and zoning out as a way of coping with stress), contacting the ground is a helpful go-to response. Place your feet flat on the ground so that you feel stable and close your eyes. If you can sit down cross-legged or lie down flat, then even better. Think of this as earthing: get as close to the ground as you can, as quickly as you can. Some studies suggest that this simple act can help reduce or relieve pain and fatigue, reduce blood pressure and improve sleep. If you're feeling disconnected from the world, this can also remind you that you belong to it and you're a crucial part of it – the ground will always be there for you.

Walking in parks and woodlands during the daytime when it's safe, or gardening in your own backyard are other powerful ways to connect with the earth.

I

BELIEVE

in

MYSELF

COME TO YOUR SENSES

A quick rule of thumb when it comes to mental health care is to move your focus from your mind to your senses. Your senses are your quickest route to getting in touch with your body and staying present-focused. When you feel yourself wobbling or becoming disorientated, name five different colours you can see, four things you can hear, three things you can smell, two things you can touch, and one thing you can taste. Alternatively, visualize moving from your head to your heart to your gut. If your heart or gut could speak, what would it say?

MASLOW'S HIERARCHY

The psychologist Abraham Maslow developed a theory about our hierarchy of needs. The idea is we cannot begin to find meaning in our lives until we have met our basic survival needs. Without food, water, safety and shelter, your life is at risk. Only when you're safe and secure can you strive for belonging and connection through friendship, romantic love or parenthood, and once those needs are met, you are free to explore your own personal life goals and hobbies, and enjoy more leisure time.

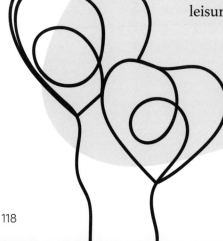

Take a moment to think about which level you're at in life. If you're trying to reach for higher goals before your foundations of nourishment and safety are set, your mental health will struggle.

"

I am here to tell you
whatever you have
believed in the past
does not have to
determine your story.

Poorna Bell

"

I
AM
SAFE

PRIORITIZE YOUR BASIC NEEDS

Your body can handle a lot, but not for too long. To function, it needs water, food, sleep and exercise. These are your baseline priorities for each and every day to help you keep your head above water.

Stay Hydrated

Research shows that dehydration can trigger the release of stress hormones, which play havoc with our mental health, while cross-sectional studies from the *World Journal of Psychiatry* show that drinking plain water is associated with a decrease in risk for depression and anxiety in adults. Aim for six to eight cups of fluid a day, which can include hot drinks, and reduce your caffeine intake.

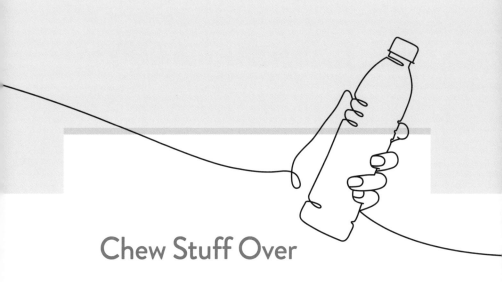

Chew Stuff Over

When we're stressed, low, anxious or depressed, it can be tempting to reach for comfort foods, which in turn leave us sluggish, and breaking that cycle gets tricky. Sugary foods make our blood-sugar levels spike, increasing our cortisol levels, causing stress and affecting our ability to manage our feelings. Try naturally sweet alternatives like cinnamon, honey or fruit. Studies also show that B vitamins are helpful toward improving your mood, but speak to your healthcare provider first to check that supplements are compatible with any medication you're taking.

SLEEP IT OFF

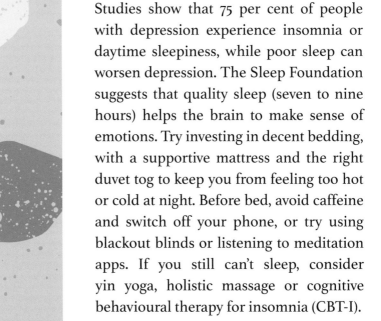

Studies show that 75 per cent of people with depression experience insomnia or daytime sleepiness, while poor sleep can worsen depression. The Sleep Foundation suggests that quality sleep (seven to nine hours) helps the brain to make sense of emotions. Try investing in decent bedding, with a supportive mattress and the right duvet tog to keep you from feeling too hot or cold at night. Before bed, avoid caffeine and switch off your phone, or try using blackout blinds or listening to meditation apps. If you still can't sleep, consider yin yoga, holistic massage or cognitive behavioural therapy for insomnia (CBT-I).

MY CHALLENGES ARE OPPORTUNITIES

GET MOVING

Clinical trials show that moving your body has huge benefits for mental health, so put on your favourite track and jump around. Aerobic exercise affects your metabolism, heart and how good you feel, reducing levels of adrenaline and cortisol in your body. It also helps to produce endorphins, feel-good hormones, which elevate your mood, reduce pain and increase feelings of relaxation. A recent study showed that regular weight training reduces anxiety, as a result of molecular changes in the muscles and brain that help lift your mood.

SELF-COMPASSION
SOOTHES THE MIND LIKE
A LOVING FRIEND WHO'S
WILLING TO LISTEN.

CHRISTOPHER GERMER

I GIVE MYSELF ROOM TO GROW

YOGA

Yoga is a spiritual practice supporting your mind-body connection and well-being at any age. This can be done at home or in a class to suit your needs. The World Health Organization (WHO) suggests that regular yoga practice can help prevent and control diseases, while its mental health benefits include focusing your mind on your breath and away from intrusive thoughts to manage anxiety and stress. Yoga styles include hatha (gentle posture and breath work), ashtanga (athletic, challenging), bikram (hot yoga), iyengar (precision and alignment), kundalini (includes chanting), restorative (prolonged postures) and yin (slow stretches).

You don't have
to understand life.
You just have to live it.

Matt Haig

I EMBRACE
MY POWER

MINDFULNESS

A stressful life can impair your immune system, interrupt your sleep and trigger low mood and irritability. Mindfulness meditation is a research-proven way to reduce this stress and in turn benefit your well-being. It influences stress pathways in the brain and changes brain activity associated with attention and emotional regulation. You can adopt mindful practices throughout your day, such as in the example below.

Mindful Walking

- Inhale deeply, and notice the fresh air fill your lungs. What can you can smell?

- As you breathe out, watch the condensation on your breath.

- Pick out the colours around you and sounds you can hear: a plane, animals rustling, the breeze... What do these evoke in you?

- Pay attention to the parts of your body you are using.

Mindfulness-Based Stress Reduction (MBSR)

MBSR is a formal therapeutic intervention combining yoga and meditation through prescribed courses and daily exercises, such as mindful eating, where you observe your experience as it's happening. Mindfulness-based cognitive behavioural therapy (MBCT) combines MBSR with CBT, which can be especially helpful if you're suffering with depression, anxiety or OCD. Speak to your doctor or therapist before trying anything new.

I

TRUST

myself

FEEL AT HOME

We can forget that our home space is as important as what we do with and put into our bodies when it comes to getting a good night's sleep or feeling calm. Making simple adjustments to your living area in order to increase your feeling of safety and security can give you huge peace of mind. This can be as big as installing locks or alarm systems in your home to put you at ease. Alternatively, you can make surface level changes to your furnishings, introduce calmer colour schemes, fabrics and smells into living space, or decorate your walls to increase your feeling of comfort at home.

GET CREATIVE

Books, TV shows, films, songs and art can all speak to us powerfully in moments of need. A favourite song or book can help us feel seen, heard and less alone in ways that sometimes people miss. Music is proven to reduce anxiety by up to 44 per cent. In fact, music therapists tell us that the music we're listening to can match our heartbeats and regulate our breathing as a natural way to ground ourselves, while neuroscience research has shown that creative improvisation like spoken poetry, rapping and storytelling increases brain activity in the medial pre-frontal cortex to help you express yourself and feel more motivated. Meanwhile, the journal *Art Therapy* suggests that 45 minutes of art-making can lower cortisol levels and therefore your stress. So harness your creative flair through writing, poetry, music making, arts and crafts, drawing or colouring in. You can do this alone or take up classes. You might even wish to have formal music, art or drama therapy with a professional to channel that part of you (see Part Five).

LISTEN TO AUDIOBOOKS OR PODCASTS

When we're low, finding the energy to socialize, entertain people or make conversation can feel like an uphill struggle, while being on our own can make us feel worse. Podcasts are a fantastic option when you're in this place. It can feel like having company in the room without any pressure to talk back. Many podcasts deal with mental health topics and offer you a chance to hear the lived experiences of other people, which can make you feel less alone. Alternatively, try an audiobook as you drift off to sleep.

Other options to turn to when you're not ready to socialize can include holistic activities that feel healing and involve you interacting with the world without any pressure for you to talk or do much back. This can be swimming, having a massage, beauty treatment or just watching the world go by in a café. Activities such as aromatherapy, acupuncture or reiki can improve your mind/body connection in a contained, safe space that ensures you're being looked after. However, always seek medical advice before trying anything that interferes with medication.

The world will see you

THE WAY YOU SEE YOU,

and treat you the way

YOU TREAT YOURSELF.

BEYONCÉ

I AM IN THE RIGHT PLACE AT THE RIGHT TIME

PART FIVE
NEXT STEPS

Sometimes, opening up isn't enough. If you think you need more formal support, this part contains resources to help you find professional help. Being fully informed about the different routes available will give you the confidence to get the support that you need. In the next few pages, you'll discover what's out there, with a guide for accessing it. It isn't easy, but once you find the right person to turn to, it can change your life.

ONE SETBACK DOESN'T UNDO MY GROWTH

YOUR THERAPY OPTIONS

Therapy can be one-to-one, with a partner or family, or in groups. It can be goal-oriented, short- or long-term, open-ended, theme specific (for example psychosexual, women's health, addiction), or group specific (e.g. LGBTQ+).

Therapy styles can be psychoanalytic and psychodynamic (focused on your childhood), humanistic (focused on your sense of self, purpose and meaning), cognitive behavioural (challenging your thoughts, behaviours and feelings), body-based (involving touch, working with emotion stored in the body), transpersonal (spiritually focused) or integrative (a mix). In psychoanalytic therapies, you'll be doing most of the talking, while humanistic therapies – gestalt, transactional analysis, person-centred and existential therapy – are more conversational. Cognitive behavioural therapies are usually shorter term and much more structured and practical.

All styles can feel challenging, but you should always feel safe. Trust your gut if you don't. Therapy is confidential, with some exceptions (see Resources).

In all honesty, therapy
has saved my life so many
times. If you're afraid to
ask for help, don't be.

Ariana Grande

IN A CRISIS

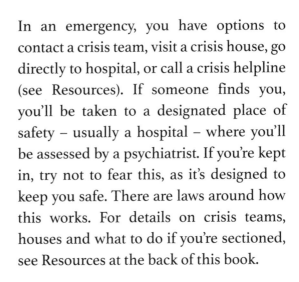

In an emergency, you have options to contact a crisis team, visit a crisis house, go directly to hospital, or call a crisis helpline (see Resources). If someone finds you, you'll be taken to a designated place of safety – usually a hospital – where you'll be assessed by a psychiatrist. If you're kept in, try not to fear this, as it's designed to keep you safe. There are laws around how this works. For details on crisis teams, houses and what to do if you're sectioned, see Resources at the back of this book.

WHO IS WHO

Psychiatrists are specialist medical doctors, who work with diagnosis and treat it with medication. Only your psychiatrist or doctor can formally diagnose you or prescribe you drugs. You'll see a psychiatrist if you're referred for psychiatric care, though you can source them privately, too. Mental health nurses work alongside psychiatrists.

Psychologists are scientists who research human behaviour – not all of them treat mental health issues, but clinical or counselling psychologists do: they have PhDs with a licence to practise, assess and create treatment plans. Clinical psychologists deliver evidence-based therapies to treat mental health symptoms, while counselling psychologists may offer additional psychotherapy approaches.

Psychotherapists and counsellors are skilled, trained professionals who help you to make sense of what you're feeling even if you don't have a formal mental health problem but you've been through something difficult, like a miscarriage or accident. Long after we lose someone, for example, people around us start to move on, but we're still left grieving. Counselling can be a safe place to take those feelings.

Licenced music, art, dance, drama and play therapists use creative mediums instead of talking. This can be helpful if you find verbal expression tricky, e.g. if you're autistic or neurodiverse in other ways.

FINDING YOUR THERAPIST

Once you know what type of therapy and professional you're after, you can ask your doctor to refer you, or self-refer through a recommendation, private insurance, or an online counselling directory (see Resources). Professional bodies usually have their own lists, such as the British Association for Counselling and Psychotherapy in the UK, the European Association for Psychotherapy in Europe, and the American Counseling Association in the US (see Resources for a more detailed list of professional bodies). If money is tight, consider counselling agencies and charities, which offer

less expensive or free options, like Mind or The Help Hub in the UK, or charities such as StrongMinds in Africa, The Jed Foundation, the Brain and Behavior Research Foundation, and National Alliance on Mental Illness in the US. Therapy training institutions also usually have lists of trainees or graduates offering therapy at lower cost. If you're a student, try your university counselling service, or if you're working for a company, check their benefits package.

A therapist will usually offer an initial call or meeting, after which you'll agree a fee and a regular slot (usually 50 minutes weekly, but this can vary).

I'VE BEEN THROUGH HARD THINGS BEFORE AND SURVIVED

"

Therapy helped
me realize that
maybe it's OK for
me to communicate
my feelings.

Kerry Washington

"

CONCLUSION

You should now have a clearer understanding of common mental health issues, how to spot them in yourself or people you love, and who to turn to for help, including ways to access more structured, professional support if you want it. You will also have loads of tips and resources to guide you along the way for your everyday self-care. Think of this book as a helpful reference to return to in times of need. The most important thing to remember is not to isolate yourself when you start feeling off balance: stay connected, let people know what's going on, and take care of your basic needs first. Feeling heard is one of the greatest gifts you can receive when it comes to your mental health. When you find the right people to turn to, this can be life-changing. You matter and we're rooting for you.

RESOURCES

Professional Bodies and Standards

American Psychiatric Association: www.psychiatry.org
American Psychological Association: www.apa.org
**British Association for Counselling and
  Psychotherapy:** www.bacp.co.uk
European Association for Psychotherapy:
  www.europsyche.org
Health and Care Professions Council: www.hcpc-uk.org
Psychological Society of South Africa:
  www.psyssa.com
**Psychotherapy and Counselling Federation
  of Australia (PACFA):** www.pacfa.org.au
United Kingdom Council for Psychotherapy:
  www.psychotherapy.org.uk

Training and guidelines for mental health practitioners differ around the world. The American Psychological Association (APA) is packed with information on practising regulations in each country, and provides a list of all the main professional bodies for psychology globally (www.apa. org/international/networks/databases).

Details on confidentiality: www.goodtherapy.org/
  blog/psychpedia/client-confidentiality
Therapy red flags: www.goodtherapy.org/
  blog/warning-signs-of-bad-therapy

Mental Health Helplines

Help Guide: www.helpguide.org/find-help.htm
Befrienders Worldwide: www.befrienders.org
For a list of worldwide suicide helplines:
  www.suicidestop.com/call_a_hotline.html

Therapy Directories

College of Sexual and Relationship Therapists, for psychosexual and relationship therapy:
www.cosrt.org.uk
Cruse, for bereavement: www.cruse.org.uk
International Therapist Directory:
https://internationaltherapistdirectory.com/online-listings/
Pink Therapy, supporting LGBTQ+:
www.pinktherapy.com

Books

Devon, Natasha, *A Beginner's Guide to Being Mental: An A–Z* (Pan Macmillan, 2018)
Grayburn, Tim, *Boys Don't Cry* (Hodder & Stoughton, 2017)
Hoare, Charlie, *Man Down: A Guide for Men on Mental Health* (Vie, 2020)
Morgan, Eleanor, *Anxiety for Beginners* (Pan Macmillan, 2016)
Sherine, Ariane, *Talk Yourself Better* (Robinson, 2018)
Van Der Kolk, Bessel, *The Body Keeps the Score* (Penguin, 2014)

Podcasts

The Likely Dads podcast, about fatherhood:
www.bbc.co.uk/programmes/m000fpcd
Mental Illness Happy Hour:podcasts.apple.com/us/
podcast/mental-illness-happy-hour/id427377900
Therapy for Black Girls podcast:
podcasts.apple.com/us/podcast/therapy-
for-black-girls/id1223803641

Charities

Worldwide

12-step programmes: www.addictioncenter.com/
treatment/12-step-programs
Addiction: atforum.com/related-websites/international-organizations
Asociación Argentina de Salud Mental: www.aasm.org.ar/es
Brain and Behaviour Research Foundation: www.bbrfoundation.org
Canadian Mental Health Association: cmha.ca
CVV (Brazil): www.cvv.org.br
Ibunda (Indonesia): www.ibunda.id
International Mental Health Charities: www.thecalmzone.net/
international-mental-health-charities; www.wheretotalk.org/charities
**Jed Foundation, teen and young adult suicide
prevention:** jedfoundation.org
**StrongMinds, treating depression in Africa for
women and young people:** strongminds.org
TalkLife, 16–24 peer-to-peer support network: www.talklife.com
Tell Japan: telljp.com/lifeline

UK

Addiction: www.actiononaddiction.org.uk
Anxiety UK: www.anxietyuk.org.uk
Beat, eating disorders: www.beateatingdisorders.org.uk

CALM, male suicide: www.thecalmzone.net

Combat Stress: www.combatstress.org.uk

Crisis, support for the homeless: www.crisis.org.uk/ending-homelessness/housing

The Maytree sanctuary if you're suicidal: www.maytree.org.uk

Mental Health Foundation, reducing stigma: www.mentalhealth.org.uk

MIND, A–Z and guidance on any mental health issue: www.mind.org.uk

OCD: www.ocduk.org

Rape Crisis: rapecrisis.org.uk

Rethink, for people severely affected by mental illness: www.rethink.org

Samaritans: www.samaritans.org, 116 123, jo@samaritans.org

Self-referral through the NHS Improving Access to Psychological Therapies (IAPT) service: www.lets-talk-iapt.nhs.uk/make-a-referral

Solace Women's Aid, domestic abuse: www.solacewomensaid.org

The US

National Alliance on Mental Illness (NAMI): www.nami.org

To Write Love On Her Arms: Depression, Addiction, Self-injury and Suicide: www.twloha.com

If you're committed:

www.treatmentadvocacycenter.org/component/content/article/183-in-a-crisis/1596-know-the-laws-in-your-state

Have you enjoyed this book?

If so, why not write a review on your favourite website?

If you're interested in finding out more about
our books, find us on Facebook at **Summersdale
Publishers**, on Twitter at **@Summersdale** and
on Instagram at **@summersdalebooks** and
get in touch. We'd love to hear from you!

Thanks very much for buying this Summersdale book.

www.summersdale.com